TAKING CONTROL

of Your Mind and Your Thoughts

2nd edition

Marybeth Wuenschel

Special thanks to Pam Criss for her contributions

Thank you to my prayer group at St. Gabriel Catholic Community, McKinney, Texas for your support and editing and to Gwen Edwards, Principal of St. Philip the Apostle Catholic School, El Campo, Texas and her teachers for being my first and faithful readers.

Taking Control 5

Strongholds 7

Negative Thoughts 12

Change Your Mind – You can 21

Depression 25

Generational Strongholds 28

You are precious to God 30

Someone had to Die 32

Sacrament of Reconciliation 38

Battle Plan How to fight 39

TOOLS FOR BATTLE 40

Tools for Battle - The Holy Spirit 41

Tools for Battle - Prayer is a weapon 42

Tools for Battle - Faith is a weapon 44

Tools for Battle-The Word is a Weapon 47

Tools for Battle -Your Mouth is a Weapon 50

Tools for Battle - Speak to Goliath 53

Tools for Battle - Jesus is our Stronghold 57

Tools for Battle - Praise is a Weapon 62

Praise as a Sacrifice 67

Praise Statements / Scriptures 68

LITANY OF PRAISE....................................72

Healing...74

Daily Proclamations 79

Taking Control

You are reading this book because you are hungry for God and want to grow in wisdom, knowledge, and truth. If you are like me, you can't get enough of Him and want to be stirred up and filled. If you are hungry, you will be filled. If you are open and have time for God, you will hear God's voice and what He has to tell you and say about you through His Holy Spirit. Get ready to be healed and renewed by the Word of God. This book is a help and not a substitute for the Word of God, for the Word of God is our sustenance, our daily bread.

The intention of this book is to make you hungry for the Word of God and God himself and introduce you to what may be standing in the way of the freedom and healing that is yours. You are in Christ, a coheir with Christ and a child of God himself. The Bible says we are more than conquerors through Christ. This book addresses strongholds and how to get out from underneath them. Jesus is our stronghold, the Bible says, and nothing else should have a hold on us. It is time to be set free because Jesus has provided the way to freedom and in Christ, we are free.

We all have strongholds we need to deal with or keep from developing. My desire is to help you recognize strongholds and learn how to break their hold and demolish them. We are overcomers and perfectly equipped for freedom from oppression. Today, let's start living like we are conquerors instead of defeated, over-comers instead of losers, alive instead of dead and free instead of the tied up, nervous, worrisome creatures we have become or are afraid we may become. We have more authority than we may know and certainly more than we are experiencing. We have more power than we understand. The Spirit that raised Jesus from the dead lives inside of you and me.

God has given us a battle plan and He is waiting to teach us how to fight for what is ours. The beginning of the victory and breakthrough is knowing that victory and breakthrough are yours and belongs to you. The battle is fought and won by knowing who you are in Christ and what you deserve.

David fought Goliath with nothing but stones and a sling. He said to Goliath, "You come against me with sword and spear and scimitar, but I come against you in the name of the Lord of hosts..." The weapons at our disposal are spiritual and just as powerful today against our giants as they were for David. Today is the day we declare our independence from whatever has a hold on us and declare our dependence on God. Jesus had given us the authority and power to break free and stay free, and our freedom begins when we realize He set us free when He went to the cross. Freedom from negative thoughts, depression, anxiety, fear, and worry is God's desire, design, and gift to us his children.

Strongholds

Do you ever let your mind wander or let your thoughts and imaginations run wild? Do you like to just let your mind go? We all do, some more than others. We were taught it's a good thing. "Let it go, let it go.... "

Our imaginations are a good thing and a gift from God. God gave us imagination so we could create, invent, conceive, play, pretend, and grow and succeed in this life. He gave us imagination so we could dream, envision, desire and wonder about Him, His creation, and His kingdom. As great and wonderful as this gift is, it is very dangerous if left unattended or allowed to run wild or out of control. Imaginations are what cause a person to believe lies about themselves such as maybe I really am perverted, maybe I really would be better off dead, maybe I am worthless, maybe the lady living next door really does hate me, etc.

Do your thoughts have control over you or do you have control over your thoughts? Who is in charge of your mind and your thoughts? Who decides what you think? Who is in charge of YOU?

There is an ongoing battle for us and a battle for our minds. The devil knows if he can get our minds he can get us.

> *"For we are not fighting against flesh-and-blood enemies, but against evil rulers and authorities of the unseen world, against mighty powers in this dark world, and against evil spirits in the heavenly places."* ***(Ephesians 6:12)***

Wickedness wants in; it's looking for an open door or an invitation. A stronghold begins with just a thought and if allowed can grow until it takes control and takes what it was never authorized to take. When a thought process has a strong hold on us, then those thoughts control us because they are more powerful than our will or ability to overthrow them. We go wherever our thoughts take us. If our thoughts are left alone or left to run amuck, we will go where we never intended to go. We will become what we were never meant to become.

Never let your mind wander. This is contrary to everything we were ever taught in school or growing up. We were taught to let our minds go and be creative. When our mind wanders, it is up for grabs, and the enemy will take advantage. He (the devil) is relentless and merciless and will seize every opportunity to gain access, take control and devour you. If you are not in control of your mind or imaginations, the devil will be happy to do it for you. **Ephesians 6:16** *"lift up the shield of faith with which you can extinguish all the flaming arrows of the evil one."* Flaming arrows are evil thoughts. Just because they come to us doesn't mean they belong to us or have to remain.

Get ready for some good news. You do not have to live with or accept every thought that comes into your mind. You are in control and master of your very own mind and thoughts. If a thought or thoughts start to bombard you, you can stop them. Your mind is yours, and it's off limits to outside forces of evil. You are in control and master of your very own mind and thoughts. You may not be able to control them coming, but you can control whether or not they take up residence.

You are an overcomer in Christ, and it doesn't matter how long you have been behaving, thinking or believing a certain way you can change your mind and therefore, more importantly, change you. You can change your future and become someone you never thought you were capable of becoming.

It doesn't matter how long you have been behaving, thinking or believing a certain way; you can change your mind and therefore, more importantly, change you. You can change your future and become someone you never thought you were capable of becoming. You can do this through Christ. He is the answer.

Our minds are very powerful. It is generally believed we are the summation of all our thoughts. What kind of thoughts went into the development of your mind, your attitude, and emotions? Were you raised with worldly or spiritual influences? We were all born and raised in this world. Jesus said to His Father regarding His disciples in John chapter 17, *"they are in the world but not of the world."* Most of us grew up both in the world and of the world. I know I did. What made us the way we are? Why are we like we are? Why do we think the way we do and react the way we do? Why do we get moody or emotional? Why are we touchy and so easily offended? What is wrong with us?

We are not meant for this world only; we are more than just physical beings, we became spiritual beings when we were born anew in Christ. Jesus said in John chapter three when He was speaking with Nicodemus, "Amen, amen, I say to you, no one can see the kingdom of God without being born from above."

If you are still reading, chances are you have been born from above into the family of God through Jesus Christ. The Catholic Church teaches that we are born anew in Christ through our baptism and that we have to choose it for ourselves at some point in our lives. You can choose Jesus Christ for yourself right now.

There is a choice set before us, the choice to continue on our own path, or to choose to remain one with him and attached to the vine.

On the back cover of this book is a prayer of surrender and commitment. Pray these prayers out loud and let the devil know and God know who you serve and worship. Choose today to be renewed in Christ Jesus. There is nothing like declaring your allegiance out loud. WORDS are powerful and effective. Your words do a ton of damage to the kingdom of Satan when you declare Jesus as your Lord. The devil hates hearing that name and for this reason, goes to great lengths to get us to misuse it.

Romans 10:9-13 *for, if you confess with your mouth that Jesus is Lord and believe in your heart that God raised him from the dead, you will be saved. For one believes with the heart and so is justified, and one confesses with the mouth and so is saved. For the scripture says, "No one who believes in him will be put to shame." For there is no distinction between Jew and Greek; the same Lord is Lord of all, enriching all who call upon him. For "everyone who calls on the name of the Lord will be saved."*

When you speak your commitment to God, you are not only announcing it in the heavenly places above and below the earth, but you are speaking to yourself as well and are assuring yourself it is true. That way you won't doubt or wonder, am I a child of God? Is God on my side? Do I really have authority over evil? Don't wonder, know! Jesus said that knowing the truth about who you are will set you free. John 8:32, "and you will know the truth, and the truth will set you free." The truth is we are set free from all forces of evil, but if we don't know it, we will continue to be enslaved.

When we accept Jesus as our Lord and Savior for ourselves and chose to love, honor and serve him, we became brand new, a new creation in Christ. YES, YOU! God made you brand new when you accepted His gift of salvation. We are new creatures, q new creations in Christ, the Bible says. We were made to live in the spirit realm. We are spirit, soul, and body and while our spirit is brand new and alive, our mind, will, and emotions (soul) need to be renewed daily.

It's very important to know who you are in Christ and what is yours. When we know who we are and what is ours, we can fight the devil and all his thoughts from a position of authority and confidence. We won't just give in or run in fear or cower and just accept things as they are. We will be willing to take back what the enemy stole from us. We become strong in the Lord and in His mighty power. Ephesians 6:10.

God wants you free of everything that has a strong hold on you. He wants you free and has made a way for you to be free from what torments you, enslaves and haunts you. You are not who your thoughts say you are! You are who God says you are!!! God wants you free of every evil thought. You are a child of the most powerful person in the universe. As you read this believe for something good to happen to you. Believe that your life is about to change for the better.

God has plans for you. Plans to take you to a new place, a better place. No matter how good or bad things are for you right now, God has better in store for you. This is nothing compared to what is coming. There is so much more coming your way. Don't settle for where you are right now.

Negative Thoughts

Not all thoughts are good. Not all thoughts are yours. Not all thoughts come from you. Negative thoughts come, but they don't have to stay. Thoughts come, but they do not have to be entertained, invited, or tolerated in any way or for any length of time. We do not have to take ownership of a thought just because it enters our mind. Many thoughts are lies. You don't have to believe them or obey them or even listen to them. This may surprise you, but many thoughts come from spiritual forces of evil.

Does the devil really exist? Do we have an enemy in heavenly places? *(Demons occupy heavenly places, not "Heaven" as we know it, which just means they are in a spiritual realm not accessible in the natural. The Bible refers to these places as heavens in Ephesians.)*

Here are some scriptural references regarding demonic forces at work against us.

> **1 John 5:19** *We know that we are children of God and that the world around us is under the control of the evil one.*

> **John 10:10** *The thief comes only to kill, steal and destroy I have come that they may have life, and have it to the full.*

> **1 Peter 5:8-9** *Stay alert, Watch out for your great enemy, the devil. He prowls around like a roaring lion, looking for someone to devour.*

> **Ephesians 6:11-12** *Put on the armor of God so that you may be able to stand firm against the tactics of the devil. For our struggle is not with flesh and blood but with the principalities, with the powers, with the world rulers of this*

present darkness, with the evil spirits in the heavens.

James 4:7 *Submit yourselves, then, to God. Resist the devil and he will flee from you.*

Col 1:13 *"For He has rescued us from the dominion of darkness and brought us into the kingdom of the Son He loves."*

May I take this opportunity to tell you something?
There is no lesson to be learned
in the pit except the way out
and Jesus is the way out.
Hang on for dear life and you will come out.

We have been raised in this world, but JESUS wants us in His world. If we have been rescued from the dominion of darkness, then the evil one has no power over us. Jesus rescued us, and He did a good job. Are you unsure about which kingdom you are living in? Let's make sure right now. Pray the "Prayer of Surrender" or the "Prayer of Commitment" right now on the back cover of this book. Read it, and it will remind you that you belong to Jesus. When you feel down or tormented or worthless or a failure regarding spiritual or worldly matters, remember that feeling does not originate from God. The devil wants to determine how we think, how we feel, and how we behave. So he places thoughts in our minds.

Isn't it a relief to know those horrible thoughts that come into your minds are not yours, and you don't have to claim them as your own or keep them. The devil will always try to drag us down.

He wants us down in the pit with him. As long as we are down in the pit or "in the gutter," he is happy and has us right where he wants us.

The devil wants us to grow in his image. Whose image are you becoming? Who do you represent? Who do you look or act like? The devil wants to tell us who we are. He wants to define us. We were not made in his image, we were made in the image of our maker. The devil hates that about us and will steal it from us if we let him.

2 Corinthians 3:18 *So all of us who have had that veil removed can see and reflect the glory of the Lord. And the Lord—who is the Spirit—makes us more and more like him as we are changed into his glorious image.*

The devil wants to be God. The devil wants you to grow in his image to spite God. If he can control what we think, he can control us. His destination for you is the pit of despair, which is where he leads and wants you to remain.

God never leads us into the pit; we do that ourselves. He neither leads us to the pit nor leaves us there. No matter how we got there or how long we have been there, His plan is always to lift us up and out. So don't believe the lies the devil is filling your mind with. Stop believing it's just your lot in life; you got yourself into this; you're stuck here; you deserve this; you are a cheater; liar; hopeless.... God lifts us up and never brings us down. It doesn't matter how many times you fail he is always there to pick you up and set you on the right course. You wouldn't still be reading this if you were a quitter. You are coming out of the pit step by step unless you give up, pack it in and quit. It's never too late for redemption, conversion, or forgiveness.
God always has time for you. You are never too much trouble for Him; He always has time for you.

Sometimes we think God has better things to do than worry about us. This is just not true. God doesn't have anything better to do than take care of you. You are that important to Him. Remember the two thieves crucified on the cross next to Jesus, only one was in his right mind and turned to Jesus. He knew it was not too late. Make Jesus' day and turn to him. Begin the journey upward.

Father I pray for the man or woman reading this right now. Speak to them, minister your love, and mercy to them. May they feel your presence and hunger and thirst for you. You promise us that we will find you when we seek you diligently. Help us be diligent.

May I take this opportunity to tell you something? There is no lesson to be learned in the pit except the way out, and the way out is Jesus. Hang on for dear life, and you will come out!!

Jesus lives. Jesus wins. We belong to Him. The devil will fill our minds with thoughts that tell us the opposite, that we don't deserve Him. But the truth is we belong to Him.

"If God is for us who can be against us." **Rom 8:31**.

"Greater is He that is in us than he that is in the world." **1 John 4:4**.

One day one of the saints of old woke up in the middle of the night and saw Satan himself standing at the foot of his bed. He woke with a start and said "Oh, it's just you! Greater is He that is in me than he that is the world" and rolled over and went back to sleep. Without Jesus, we are at the mercy of principalities, and the spiritual forces of evil. With Jesus, we are more than conquerors. We can overcome anything. We are no longer trapped. So step out into freedom.

Here are some examples of negative thoughts we entertain, thoughts we file away, hold onto and eventually believe about ourselves.

I am a failure.	I am a bad mother/father.	I'll never get it right.
I am useless.	No one likes me.	No one needs me.
I will have cancer.	I am going to get sick and die.	I will grow old all alone.
No one will take care of me.	God doesn't have time for me.	He doesn't care about me.
I am perverted.	I will not have enough money.	I am fat, ugly, old.

Here are some other examples of negative thoughts or attitudes we practice. These words come out of our mouths so readily because we think them all the time. These thoughts occupy our mind and have become our default thoughts, and therefore they show up or will in our everyday language.

I hate my life... I hate my clothes, my house.	How dare she...	Who does he think he is....
She makes me sick.	What a jerk.	I deserve better.
He makes me crazy.	It's all her fault.	I hate her. I hate him....

These thoughts cannot reside in us, or we will become as ugly as they sound. They will literally make us sick. We need to undo/recall/delete/erase/unlearn these habitual thoughts.

This may be news to you, but we do not have to allow negative thoughts to invade the privacy of our brains. Our minds are OURS! Are you ready to take back what is yours and take control and ownership of your very own mind? It is that simple. Jesus said we could, and he has equipped us with the power and authority to do it. We don't have to allow a thought in any more than we have to allow a stranger, a burglar, a pig or a snake into our home.

How? How do we do it?

First, we have to recognize and separate good thoughts from bad, the devil's thoughts from your own. I have listed common thoughts so you will know that you are not alone. Others think the same way. I have listed them so you will also know which thoughts to stay away from; which are not of God and therefore you should not be meditating on.

Secondly, we have to believe it's possible. The Bible says in Philippians chapter 4 to think a certain way. If God tells us what to think about, then it must be doable. There is a way to stop the bad thoughts and keep them from entering.

Phil 4:8 *Fix your thoughts on what is true, and honorable, and right, and pure, and lovely, and admirable. Think about things that are excellent and worthy of praise.*

Thirdly, we have to be committed. Fear and worry will not give up without a fight. How committed are you? Will you cave the first sign of push back? The fear that has held you for so long will not leave unless it knows and believes you are serious and mean what you say.

Recurring thoughts that we entertain become strongholds. They have a foothold and have taken up residence and are not willing to just pick up and leave because you say so. Depression, for example, is a stronghold and evil. Worry, anxiety and doubt are not just going to run when they see you coming with a new conviction. They will test your resolve. Moodiness, sickness, jealousy, addictions, rage, and temper tantrums.

Worry - to feel anxious about something unpleasant that may have happened or may happen; To torment oneself with disturbing thoughts

These are all examples of strongholds that were never meant to become part of who we are. We were not made this way. We were made for better attitudes, emotions, and a stable mind. You have to believe there is better for you or you won't get fear to believe you and obey you. You have to know, that as a child of God you have authority to command these wicked thoughts to leave you. You have authority because Jesus gave it to you. You don't deserve this anymore if Jesus has forgiven you. The accuser has nothing to accuse you of. As long as you believe you don't deserve the freedom, you will never receive it.

Lastly, we have to act.

Would You Let a Snake Stay?

Just because you find a snake in the middle of your living room doesn't mean it has to stay there. Just because it got in doesn't mean it has to be fed and entertained. We don't wine and dine unwanted guests. If you came home and found a snake in the middle of your living room would you tell your family that they just have to deal with it? Would you say "you're just going to have to get used to it, live with it?" Would you tell your children to try to stay out of its way? NO! You would chop off its head. We don't live with snakes, so why live with strongholds (depression, anger, fear, insecurity, hatred....). They want us, they want to control us, but they can't have us.

I read a book once called "Pigs in the Parlor." It was about the devil and his demons taunting us. It describes demon activity against Christians this way. Imagine you have pigs in your parlor or dining room. What are you going to do? Are you going to ask them to leave, beg them to leave, cry, and complain? Do you entertain them and keep cleaning up after them, do you tolerate or ignore them hoping they will just go away or are you going to drive them out?

2 Corinthians 10:3-5
For though we live in the world, we do not wage war as the world does. The weapons we fight with are not the weapons of the world. On the contrary, they have divine power to demolish strongholds. We demolish arguments and every pretension that sets itself up against the knowledge of God, and we take captive every thought to make it obedient to Christ.

COMMAND your thoughts into obedience like the Bible tells you to. You are in charge. It is your mind after all. TRY IT. Don't be shy. Say out loud "Memories, thoughts, leave me! There is a new sheriff in town, his name is Jesus. Jesus is Lord of my mind. I command you to go in the name of my Lord Jesus." Jesus left us His name. Don't be afraid to use it.

Change Your Mind – You can

Every time a thought or a memory comes to mind we have a choice to reinforce it or dismiss it. When a negative, hurtful or otherwise evil thought or memory is not cast out or nipped in the bud we start believing it and agreeing with it. We can entertain them or cast them out. We can make room for them or kick them out. We can invite them to spend the night or drive them away. If we dwell on negative thoughts and allow them to set up camp in our minds they will take up residence and become a stronghold that is not easily broken, healed or overcome.

> It doesn't matter how long you have been behaving, thinking or believing a certain way, you can change your mind and therefore, more importantly, change you.

Our brain knows how to store thoughts and save them, filing them, and even prioritizing them based on the amount of time we spend thinking about them. It is chemistry. We don't have to follow our thoughts. Our minds can be changed, redirected and refocused. We can change what we think about. The definition of mind according to Webster is....the element or complex of elements in an individual that feels, perceives, thinks, wills, and especially reasons. Our minds are our conscious and unconscious mental activity. I want my mind, my emotions, my perceptions and automatic responses to be ruled and developed by me and my God, not by a whim or misguided directive.

We can change the way we think and what we think about and if God tells us what to think about as he does in Philippians then it must be doable.

Philippians 4:8 *Finally, brethren, whatever things are true,* *whatever things are noble, whatever things are just, whatever things are pure, whatever things are lovely, whatever things are of good report, if there is any virtue and if there is anything praiseworthy meditate on these things.*

We cannot think about two things at the same time, so if you don't like where your thoughts are going change your mind by choosing to think of something else. Ask the Holy Spirit for help. Ask Him to show you when you are going down that path that leads to "Funkville." Ask the Holy Spirit to warn you, to give you an opportunity to see and to recognize when you are about to spiral or lash out. Your mind right now has a default that needs to be reset. You have been reacting the same way for so long it takes an effort to reset it. But it will obey. Don't give up.

The Holy Spirit wants to walk with you and have a relationship with you. He is there for you. He doesn't have better things to do than help you. You are His desire.

IT'S JUST A THOUGHT!!!!

Thoughts are just that, thoughts. We can be driven by them, worried by them, terrorized and controlled by them. They are what the Bible calls in Ephesians 6 flaming arrows of the evil one. He plants thoughts in our minds keep us down and out. He is merciless and when he finds which thoughts work he won't let up. Once we realize they are just thoughts we can dismiss them or command them into obedience.

Once I was on an airplane from Dallas to Cleveland and I began to panic. I saw myself in steel tube in the sky. I started to freak out. I had to get to the back of the plane and practically pushed my way to the restroom. I started to hyper-ventilate and had a vision of myself lying on the floor foaming at the mouth. I kept praying and saying "Please Lord help me, I trust you." I kept repeating it as I waited for the lavatory. I got in front of the mirror and looked at myself and I heard the Holy Spirit say "It's just a thought." It's just a thought; yes it's just a thought! I am not going to be taken down by a thought!!! I looked at myself and commanded my thoughts into obedience. I said "Thoughts, I command you into obedience. I command you to obey Jesus. Jesus is my Lord and Lord of my mind." Immediately I was fine and went back to my seat and sat down without a trace of fear or worry.

JUST CHANGE YOUR MIND

Another day we were in the car on our way to church. Thoughts came and began to overwhelm me. Words began to well up inside of me. If they didn't come out I was going to burst. It was lecture time. My children needed to know what I expected from them that day and they needed to know it now, on our way to church. If I didn't tell them what to expect when we get home, all hope would be lost. The usual crazy impulse came and right before I began the lecture that would ruin the morning for all of us I recognized that the thought didn't need to move me. I realized for the first time that I could just not go there. I chose to dismiss the thought, the whole argument.

Finally I was listening to the Lord instead of the usual tirade of thoughts. He gave me a second to see, a chance to make it right. It was so clear to me that I was about to ruin a perfectly wonderful morning. I decided at that moment that I would not let that thought rule. I just turned it off and trusted God. It was so nice to see it happen, to see it become a reality.

Thank you Holy Spirit for showing me and giving me that chance to choose. Ask the Holy Spirit to give you a chance to choose correctly. Thoughts and reactions to thoughts have become automatic we have lived that way for so long.

Ask the Holy Spirit to give you a chance to do the right thing. I used to fly off the handle with my kids. I was following the Lord and had surrendered my life to him but still would fail more often than win. I was rude to my husband and mean to my mother. I couldn't seem to stop myself. Before I knew it the words were out and the damage was done. I felt like a failure. I had no time to make a good decision. I was on auto pilot and out of control. A friend told me to ask the Holy Spirit to put a check in my spirit. Even a few seconds is enough to stop the response that comes automatically. Ask the Holy Spirit to give you a chance to respond correctly. He did for me. He truly is our helper. He wants you to succeed and is here to help you do just that. Call on him. He is our helper, our ever present help in time of need, the bible says in Psalm 46:1.

Ask the Holy Spirit to reveal to you the traps the devil has set up for you; the triggers that set you off. You have been on automatic but not for long. You are a new creature and God has transferred you out of the darkness and into the son he loves. He will transform you into the real you. The YOU, you were created to be.

Romans 12:2 *Don't copy the behavior and customs of this world, but let God transform you into a new person by changing the way you think. Then you will learn to know God's will for you, which is good and pleasing and perfect.*

Depression

" Thoughts are like trains" someone once said. "They take you somewhere." One thought leads to another, and if your thoughts are negative, you will soon end up in a place called "FUNKVILLE." The more you follow a thought to Funkville the easier it is to get there. You lose control. One little thought or memory can trigger the downward spiral, and soon you are full speed ahead to Funkville. If you do end up in Funkville, don't stay there. There is a way out.

You were not made to handle Funkville so don't stay. It may have become a comfortable place for you. You may have been there so long you don't know how to leave, or you may have lost directions home. FUNKVILLE is not God's design or desire for you; it is not God's destination for you ever. God has the ticket out, and it is yours for free.

FUNKVILLE, it's Not God's Will or Plan for Your Life

Depression comes from many different sources but no matter where it comes from or how it got there it is time for it to hit the road. I believe depression is the devil's favorite tool against the body of Christ. No matter how long you have lived with it or how "clinical" or "medical" it is, it is time for it to go. It is not God's will or plan for your life. Believe that.

You may have it bad, and it may be quite serious, but know that its hold over you has been conquered, demolished, the chains have been loosed, and the straps that have bound you have been severed. You have been set free, and it is time to receive that freedom and walk in it. This freedom comes with faith and trust in the One that set you free. It is happening one day at a time or all at once, but it IS happening.

One definition of depression is this, "determination to reach a goal that is impossible to achieve." I was telling this to my neighbor. I told her "one definition for depression is the determination or compulsion to reach a goal that is impossible to achieve." She said, "Oh, you mean like, I can never be a grandma because my only daughter just had a complete hysterectomy?" Yes. Depression is to be routed and overthrown and today is the day. Not tomorrow, but today. It is time to be rescued by your knight in shining armor, JESUS. It's time to lift up your arms to the rescuer and trust him to come for you. WAIT for the Lord, wait expectantly, for he shall surely come (Psalm 27:14). The world may say you are stuck with it, you are in too deep, but God says that those who hope in HIM will renew their strength.

God goes on to say *"they will soar on wings like eagles, they will run and not grow weary, they will walk and not grow faint"* **(Isaiah 40:31). Psalm 18:8** says *"They confronted me in the day of my disaster, but the Lord was my support."*

This is for you, not just your neighbor or the holy woman who sits next to you in the pew; it is for YOU. It may not come tomorrow, but it will happen. Don't give up and don't quit believing. Strongholds, like depression, are not easily destroyed but praise God we are more than conquerors through Christ Jesus. If you are in Christ, if Christ lives in you and He does, or you wouldn't be reading this book, then you are a conqueror. You have a conquering spirit in you. Depression is not tolerated, it is conquered. The Bible says that EVERYTHING is possible for those who believe. Are you a believer? Do you want to go boldly where you have never gone before? You can and you will.

>**Col 1:13** *"For He has rescued us from the dominion of darkness and brought us into the kingdom of the Son He loves."*

Jesus didn't rescue us just to see us miserable and in a pit. He didn't set us free to see us in bondage. We are no longer at the mercy of our past, our thoughts, our memories, our dreams/ nightmares. We are no longer at the mercy of our attitudes. We are over-comers.

> **Luke 10:19** *I have given you authority to trample on snakes and scorpions and to overcome all the power of the enemy.*

Generational Strongholds

Some Strongholds are passed down through generations

Sin, if not dealt with is passed down from father to son, mother to daughter, grandfather to granddaughter, etc. Sin may come to you through your ancestors, but it doesn't have to remain in you. Sin is sin and must be dealt with. Jesus dealt with sin, your sin and your parent's sin, yesterday's sins, today's sins and tomorrow's sins. Confess your sins. Do not live with them and tolerate them. We like to blame our ancestors because for some reason it makes us feel better and also gives us permission to keep those certain habits/sins. Sin is sin, whether you were born that way or not. Just because your bad temper came from your ancestors is not a license to rage.

We say things like:
      "It's just the way I am"
      "God made me this way"
      "Deal with it"

We say or think such things as:
      "It runs in my family"
      "It's in my genes"
      "We are Italian after all"
      "Everybody drinks in my family, we're Irish"
      "My mother had breast cancer and so did her mother before her"
      "I was born homosexual, it's just who I am"

We may have been born with those tendencies, but we don't have to remain that way. There is no way out if you think it is just the way you are. There is no forgiveness if you don't recognize sin as sin.

Ready for some earthshaking, mind-blowing good news? If Jesus said we are born again, then we are born again, free of every generational curse that has been following us through our bloodline. If that is not good enough, there is more! It will not go any further. It stops with you. It will not be passed down to your children unless you let it; unless you accept it as 'just the way it is.' We have a new bloodline; a new heritage; a new ancestry. We were born again and transferred into the Kingdom of the Son where we are coheirs with Christ.

Ephesians 3:6 *This mystery is that through the gospel the Gentiles are heirs together with Israel, members together of one body, and sharers together in the promise in Christ Jesus.*

Jesus says we are new creations.

> *"If anyone is in Christ he is a new creation, the old has gone, the new has come"* **2 Corinthians 5:17**

These aren't just words. This is the truth. In Christ, we are brand new. In Him we are born again, new creations, molded and shaped in His image. You have the opportunity today to be the YOU God created YOU to be. God has you in mind, and He is molding you into the noble, respectable, gracious, wise, pure, kind, generous, heroic, fine, person of integrity with a heart for God.

You don't have to remain that timid, fearful, easily offended, critical, worried person anymore. You also do not have to remain trapped in sinful behavior. It is not "the way you are." You are no longer like that.

"There is neither Jew nor Greek, slave nor free, male nor female, for you are all one in Christ Jesus. If you belong to Christ, then you are Abraham's seed, and heirs according to the promise."
Galatians 3:28-29

You are precious to God

Isaiah 49 :15-16 *Never! Can a mother forget her nursing child? Can she feel no love for the child she has borne? But even if that were possible, I would not forget you! See, I have written your name on the palms of my hands.*

You are precious to God. You matter to Him more than you know. You are worth more to Him than you can ever imagine. He loves you so much he gave up His Son for you. If you were the only person on earth, God would have sent His Son to die just for you. That is how much he loves and cherishes you. He knows the number of hairs on your head. God has your name written on His hand. He says this in Isaiah 49.

Why do we doubt His love for us? We do! If we were really honest with ourselves, we would realize just how unsure we are of His love and devotion to us. We doubt He will be with us when we need Him; we doubt we will be taken care of in our old age. We doubt, but God demands our faith in His love for us. God wants you to believe and trust in His love for you. It's not enough to believe God exists; God expects you and me to believe not just that He exists, even the devil believes that, but that He loves us unconditionally. He went to great lengths to prove His love.

Romans 5:8 *But God proves his love for us in that while we were still sinners Christ died for us.*

God proved He loved us by sending Jesus to die in our place. What an act of love. He did it so you and I would never doubt His love for us. Yet we doubt. If God sending His son to die doesn't prove to you He loves you, than nothing will. Some might give their life for a noble purpose or for a special loved one, but God sent Jesus to die for us while we were sinners, proving His love for us. He didn't wait for us to get our act together. No. He loves you and me just the way we are.

We are worth everything to Him. The fact that God loves us, sins and all is what makes God so special. He already chose you and me. He chose us before time began.

Ephesians 1:4 *as he chose us in him, before the foundation of the world.*

He didn't wait to see what we would be like before he decided to send his Son to die. He already knows us and wants us, sins and all. It's so hard for us to believe because we would be a different kind of God. God's ways are not our ways. God has already done it and now it's up to you to believe he did it just for you. He sent Jesus to the cross for you and me while we were sinners! This fact is paramount. This is the proof of his love for you right now. You were a sinner when he chose you. There is nothing you can do to change his mind about you. He already made up his mind when he sent Jesus. He sent Jesus to die for sinners, that included you and me. So when you sin, does God love you less? He loved you before you were born. He loved you before you could earn his love. He decided to love you while you were still a sinner. This was on purpose. He wanted you to never doubt His love for you. He wanted you to remember His love especially when you just sinned. God is worthy of praise. He is just so good.

God has determined our value; we are priceless to Him. We are worth more to God than even Jesus. He sacrificed Jesus so he could have us. NOW LISTEN TO THIS! God sacrificed His only Son without any assurance anyone would accept this sacrifice. He sacrificed Jesus knowing many would not even notice or care. God was willing to give his Son Jesus even if no one chose to receive this gift. That's how valuable you are to Him.

Someone had to Die

Someone had to die. The Bible says that the wages of sin is death (**Romans 6:23)**. You sin, you die. In the garden God told Adam and Eve, if you eat the fruit of the tree of Knowledge, you will certainly die. They died a spiritual death that day and along with them, the whole human race. God and sin do not mix. God is a loving God but also a just God. The only way we can be free from sin is for someone to DIE in our place. Jesus brought us back to life by dying for us. He took the death punishment meant for us.

Romans 6:23 *For the wages of sin is death. but the gift of God is eternal life in Christ Jesus.*

You sin, you die. In the garden God told Adam and Eve, if you eat the fruit of the Tree of Knowledge, you will certainly die. They died a spiritual death that day and along with them, the whole human race. God and sin do not mix. God is a loving God but also a just God. The only way we can be free from sin is for someone to DIE in our place. Jesus brought us back to life by dying for us. He took the death punishment meant for us.

Jesus became the sacrificial Lamb of God for us because he really and truly loves us. That is why we call him the Lamb of God. In the Old Testament, an altar was erected in the Tabernacle that Moses built according to God's instructions. On the altar, day and night sacrifices were made for the sins of the people. Lambs and bulls and goats were slaughtered, and the blood of the animals was poured on the altar and covered the sins of the people. These animals died in place of the people. On the Day of Atonement, the High Priest went into the Holy Of Holies, the place where no one but the High Priest could enter, and even then only once a year on the Day of Atonement. The High Priest went in to offer the blood of the sacrifice for the sins of the nation. This blood was required to purify the Tabernacle/Temple.

These sacrifices were a foreshadowing of the true Lamb of God that was coming to take away the sins of the world. Jesus is the lamb that was slain for us, and his blood went into the "MOST HOLY PLACE" heaven, and Jesus himself, our High Priest, presented to God the Father as the atoning sacrifice for the sins of the world, His very own blood. God accepted Jesus' gift of himself; God accepted Jesus' blood in exchange for our lives.

Hebrews 9:22 *According to the law almost everything is purified by blood, and without the shedding of blood there is no forgiveness.*

Jesus is the true Lamb of God. God required not just any lamb from the people but the unblemished lambs. God expected from the people their best. This too was a foreshadowing of Jesus who was the only one who could keep the law and truly be an unblemished offering for the sins of the people. He was sinless and therefore the perfect Lamb of God, the perfect, unblemished Lamb.

When he sacrificed himself for us, He not only took our sins from us but exchanged natures with us. He became sin so we could become righteous. He did not just take sin away but changed us. He gave us a new nature, a righteous nature.

2 Corinthians 5:21 *For our sake he made him to be sin who did not know sin, so that we might become the righteousness of God in him.*

2 Corinthians 5:17 *So whoever is in Christ is a new creation: the old things have passed away; behold, new things have come.*

He gave us new hearts, hearts cleansed; hearts that long for him and hearts that want to do his will (Ezekiel 36:26). We are new creations. We are spirit, soul and body and while our spirit is brand new and alive, our mind, will and emotions (soul) need to be renewed daily. We truly become brand new when we choose him for ourselves. Our parents may have chosen Christ for us when we were baptized, but at some point, we have to choose him for ourselves. This is when everything changes. You are a brand new creation in him. The seed planted in you at Baptism comes to life when you choose Christ for yourself and taking the Eucharist becomes a brand new, life changing experience.

Jesus became sin for us and took the cross that He didn't deserve so we could become right with God and receive life and all the blessings God intended for us. God gave Israel the Law to obey promising them life and blessings if they observed ALL he commanded.

If they chose to obey God, they would be blessed by God. **Deuteronomy 28:2** *All these blessings will come upon you and overwhelm you when you obey the voice of the Lord, your God:*

If they chose not to obey they would be cursed. **Deuteronomy 28:15** *But it shall come to pass, if you do not obey the voice of the Lord your God, to observe carefully all His commandments and His statutes which I command you today, that all these curses will come upon you and overtake you:*

God, knowing we could not keep his commandments, made a way for us to gain every blessing He promised us - Jesus. Jesus obeyed for us. Jesus is God's gift to us, the gift that brings life and blessing.

Galatians 3:13-14 *Christ ransomed us from the curse of the law by becoming a curse for us, for it is written, "Cursed be everyone who hangs on a tree," ¹⁴ that the blessing of Abraham might be extended to the Gentiles through Christ Jesus, so that we might receive the promise of the Spirit through faith.*

Read Deuteronomy 28:1-14 to learn about the blessings of obedience Jesus earned for us by His obedience unto death. Read Deuteronomy 28:15-end to learn of the curses for disobedience Jesus took for us. He took the full brunt for us.

God's love is beyond our human understanding.

We don't know what love is apart from Him. He is love. He is the author of Love. We love because he first loved us. Because of his love for us, we can love everyone and anyone. His love is in us, and it is a consuming love; a love that transforms us into the lovers of humankind through him. Once we receive his love, we have no excuse not to love. We have been given the power and grace to love and forgive.

1 John 4:19 *We love because he first loved us.*

He is unchanging; he doesn't change his mind about us because we sin or forget about him. He doesn't love us because of our goodness or our abilities; he just loves us because we are His.

God cannot love you any more than he does at this very moment. God does not love you more if you do good deeds or less if you fail to. There is nothing you can do to earn His love except only receive it. To turn to him and trust Him. God cannot love you any less than he does right now. He doesn't love you more or less based on your behavior or actions. He doesn't love you less when you sin no matter how grievous.

There is no getting away from Him. There is nothing that can separate you from Him because you are in Jesus Christ. Jesus took away the sin that separates you and me from God. Jesus came between God and us with the Cross, and through Him, we have an open door to the throne room of God.

John 15:13 *There is no greater love than to lay down one's life for one's friends.*
John 3:16 *says, For God so loved the world that he gave his one and only Son, that whoever believes in him shall not perish but have eternal life.*

The Bible says that "*There is therefore now no condemnation to those who are in Christ Jesus, who do not walk according to the flesh, but according to the Spirit.*" **(Romans 8:1).** The Bible does not say that there is now no condemnation for those who are perfect.

Today we come boldly to GOD the Father through Jesus Christ. We come boldly and confidently because our hope is not in what we have done but in what Jesus has done. This is why we come in confidence. We have no confidence coming in our own strength or goodness. That will always fail us or betray us. But Jesus was perfect, and He perfectly fulfilled every commandment for us. He gave us his perfection. He gave us his right to enter the Holy of Holies. He gave us what he earned, not what we deserve. He did it all for us.

ONCE UPON A TIME

In the 4th century AD in Korea a man had two sons. The elder rose to become Chief Justice in the land and the younger became an infamous bandit. The elder brother loved his younger brother but was unable to persuade him to change his ways.

Eventually the younger son was caught and brought before his brother, the Chief Justice. Everyone in the courtroom thought the younger brother would get off because it was well known that the Chief Justice loved his brother but at the end of the trial, the Chief Justice sentenced his brother to death.

On the day of the execution, the elder brother came to the prison and said to his brother "Let's swap places." The younger brother agreed thinking that once they realized that it was the elder brother, the execution would not go forward.

On he went up on the hill to watch the proceedings. His brother was brought out at dawn and to his horror executed.
Filled with remorse, he ran down the hill and told the guard his name and that he was the criminal who should be executed. The guards said to him.

"There is no sentence outstanding on anyone with that name"

This is the case for those who choose Christ. There is no sentence outstanding. Our sins have been done away with.

Isaiah 1:18 *Come now, let us set things right,*
says the Lord:Though your sins be like scarlet,
they may become white as snow; Though they be red like
crimson, they may become white as wool.
1 John 1:9 *If we acknowledge our sins, he is faithful and just*
and will forgive our sins and cleanse us from every
wrongdoing.
Psalm 103:12 *As far as the east is from the west,*
so far has he removed our sins from us.

Sacrament of Reconciliation

James 5:16 *Therefore, confess your sins to one another and pray for one another, that you may be healed.*

The Sacrament of Reconciliation is a gift and offers us the opportunity to come before God and man and confess our sins, knowing fully that He already forgave us at the cross; knowing fully that we are forgiven. What a gift. It isn't a law or an obligation; it is a "Get To." we simply get to go to Confession. What an opportunity the Church offers us. God isn't waiting to forgive; he already made the decision to forgive us 2000 years ago. He doesn't say YES and or NO! He simply says yes when we come to him with the heart of repentance.

So confess your sins to one another and be free and healed. If there is a sin that is bothering you, that is causing you stress and agitation, confess it to someone you trust. If you are Catholic I recommend confession. You will leave lighter and free from guilt because the devil will no longer be able to accuse you. Once it's confessed, he has no hold on you.

This is an excerpt from Kate Johnston's teaching on Justification...

> As humans, we all sin, and our sins have consequences that must be dealt with. God is aware of all of our sins and offers forgiveness through the death of His Son on the cross. We can either accept God's gift of salvation and eternal life, through FAITH IN HIS SON or, we can reject this gift and suffer God's ultimate judgment. The choice is ours to make. God desires we all accept and receive His forgiveness. As Catholics, we have the opportunity to receive grace and forgiveness in the Sacrament of Reconciliation.

Battle Plan How to fight

2 Cor 10: 3-5 *"For though we live in the world, we do not wage war as the world does. 4 The weapons we fight with are not the weapons of the world. On the contrary, they have divine power to demolish strongholds. 5 We demolish arguments and every pretension that sets itself up against the knowledge of God, and we take captive every thought to make it obedient to Christ."*

The weapons at our disposal are spiritual, and they are powerful because when we use them, we have all the power of heaven behind us. Just like David had when he went up against Goliath, you too have spiritual forces behind you. You, like David, are armed. Listen to what the Bible says about the battle.

2 Chronicles 20:15 *The Lord says to you: Do not fear or be dismayed at the sight of this vast multitude, for the battle is not yours but God's.*
2 Chronicles 20:17 *You will not have to fight in this encounter. Take your places, stand firm, and see the salvation of the Lord; He will be with you, Judah and Jerusalem. Do not fear or be dismayed.*
1 Samuel 17:37 *David continued: "The same Lord who delivered me from the claws of the lion and the bear will deliver me from the hand of this Philistine."*
1 Samuel 17:47 *All this multitude, too, shall learn that it is not by sword or spear that the Lord saves. For the battle belongs to the Lord, who shall deliver you into our hands."*

Ready for the Battle plan? Here are your tools and with them a strategy for overcoming anything and everything coming against you.

TOOLS FOR BATTLE

The Holy Spirit
Prayer
Faith
Word of God (The Bible)
Mouth - Speak
Jesus is our Stronghold
Praise

Tools for Battle - The Holy Spirit

Recognize the enemy.
The Holy Spirit will help us to recognize a stronghold. The first step to victory and freedom is knowing what we are fighting and recognizing it as evil.

As long as we think this stronghold is just a part of who we are, then we will never be rid of it. What gets you down? What keeps you up at night, what consumes you, eats you up inside, what eats your lunch day after day?

Do you want to keep fighting this yourself or are you ready to let Jesus fight your battle for you? It is His battle to fight, not yours. He is our fortress, our deliverer. Ask the Holy Spirit to show you what enslaves you. He will show us the stronghold(s) in our lives if we want Him to. Ask the Holy Spirit. He is our Helper, "our ever-present help in time of need," the Bible says so.

If you don't know whether or not you have a stronghold, ask the Holy Spirit, do not try to investigate on your own. He will point them out, don't worry. The Holy Spirit is really good at it; it is His job. He will do it gently and perfectly. He has ONLY your best interest at heart.

Recognizing you have an enemy is half the battle. Once you realize you have an enemy and he wants to control you, you will want to fight.

Tools for Battle - Prayer is a weapon

James 5:16-18 *"the prayer of the righteous is powerful and effective."* **Matthew 18:19-20** *"Again, I tell you that if two of you on earth agree about anything you ask for, it will be done for you by my Father in heaven. For where two or three gather together in my name, there am I with them."*

When we pray, we are admitting to God that we need Him. Prayer is an act of humility. When we ask others to pray for us, we humble ourselves before God and others, and when we do, He promises in His word to exalt us **(1 Peter 5:5-7).** What a great God we serve.

> **Merriam-Webster defines prayer as** (1) an address (as a petition) to God or a god in word or thought (2) an earnest request or wish.
>
> Jesus said in **Matthew chapter 7:7-8** *"Ask, and it will be given to you; seek, and you will find; knock, and it will be opened to you. For everyone who asks receives, and he who seeks finds, and to him who knocks it will be opened."*

Pray! Ask! Ask and keep on asking. Ask big, ask small, and just ask so that God can get the glory. If we don't ask, we don't have an opportunity to praise God. One day on the way home from my son's baseball game, my husband Mark suggested we go to Nissan of McKinney. That summer they gave away a car every Friday night. I did not want to go, my head was throbbing, and I said: "no, not really." He continued, "They also have free food." I said okay, and on the way, we prayed for favor in the raffle. We prayed "God if it's Your will we are asking for favor in this raffle in the name of Jesus." Who knows, we could have been the only family who prayed that night. We won the car. When I saw the car being raffled, I said: "This is my car." It turned out I was right.

We had been looking for a car for the last two weeks but kept coming up against roadblocks We prayed in the parking lot before going in to each dealership and just felt a lack of peace each time.

Finally, that very Friday morning, Mark said, "Marybeth, I believe the reason we can't find a car is because God wants to give us one." That very evening we won the car. I praise God for that car all the time and tell the story often. I tell it to give God glory. What you have to know is we, Mark and I, do not deserve this car anymore than you do. God has no favorites. ASK and you too will have a story to tell. God has taught me so much through this car and a true gem is this, if God cares about giving me a car, how much more will He take care of my health or my children or anything else I give him.

James 4:2 *"You do not have because you do not ask."*

Prayer without faith is a useless tool/weapon. It is like having a security system installed and leaving it off because you just don't believe it actually works. My friend used to say "pray believing prayers or don't pray at all." When you pray, act like you just prayed. Act like you believe God heard you and is working on your behalf. So many times we pray and then go right back to worry, fear and doubt. Don't complain change your talk. Instead of complaining about how sick you are, tell yourself and others around you, "I am well; Jesus heard my prayer and has healed me. I believe I am well and this illness is running from me." Persevere, it may not seem like it, but God is working. Trust and hang in there. You are coming out victorious.

Tools for Battle - Faith is a weapon

Ephesians 6:16 *Take up the shield of faith, with which you can extinguish all the flaming arrows of the evil one.*

Jesus was amazed at the faith of the Canaanite woman and the faith of the Centurion. Jesus will be amazed at your faith in Him. Be bold as you come to God for prayer. Be like a little child asking his or her mommy or daddy to kiss it and make it better. That little child has no doubt in his/her parents' desire to fix it. Why do we doubt God's desire to make it all better for us, His children? He wants us to approach Him like you want your little children to approach you, with confidence that you not only can but will. Imagine waking your son or daughter up in the morning and finding him in bed with a festering wound, and he says, "Oh Mom/Dad I didn't want to bother you." How would you feel?

The Bible says *let's approach the throne of grace with confidence, so that we may receive mercy and find grace to help us in our time of need* (**Hebrews 4:16**). God cares about everything, even about the little things. God says *"Cast all your cares on me because I care for you"* (***1 Peter 5:7***).

Learn to do it. Practice it today. Cast your cares on HIM. He can handle it. As a matter fact, you cannot handle it, but He can. Practice with the little things, and when the big one comes you will be ready, you will know who to go to, and you will go with confidence like David did. David wasn't afraid of Goliath he had killed the bear and the lion while he tended the sheep. God wants ALL your cares not just some of them.

Now believe it!!! Jesus says *"Therefore I tell you, whatever you ask for in prayer, believe that you have received it, and it will be yours."* **Mark 11:24**

Believe that God has heard your prayers, that He is on your side and fighting your battles for you. Believe that whatever you ask for in prayer you have received.
Jesus says in **John 14:12-14**, *"I tell you the truth, anyone who has faith in me will do what I have been doing. He will do even greater things than these, because I am going to the Father. 13 And I will do whatever you ask in my name, so that the Son may bring glory to the Father. 14 You may ask me for anything in my name, and I will do it."*

Believe you are worth it. YOU ARE WORTH IT to God. Don't listen to the accuser, the liar, or the thoughts running around in your brain that want you to doubt or question. God has a message for you. He loves you and cares about you. Sometimes it is so hard to believe God cares and is working on our behalf especially when the prayer isn't answered right away. You may have to wait a short while or a long while, but He IS working. Trust that the wait will be worth it.

There is nothing preventing your prayers from being answered except your lack of trust and faith in Him. If there is unconfessed sin in your life, HE will let you know, and you will have the opportunity to confess and bring it to the light. Don't worry about sin keeping you from receiving something from God. If it is, the Holy Spirit will let you know. The Holy Spirit will expose it; He will not leave you in the dark. You will have the opportunity to reject that sin and move on. There is nothing you have done that He hasn't seen before in someone else, so confess it and get over it and begin walking again. He has already forgiven you so receive your forgiveness, don't hold on to your sins and remain in guilt and shame.

Jesus loves you so much He died for you. He died for you, so let it count. Don't let Jesus' death on the cross be in vain, let Him take ALL your sins, He wants them, we were not meant to carry them. The price He paid for you is beyond measure because you are worth everything to HIM. Don't rob Jesus of YOU. You were His reward, His prize for taking the cross. He won the battle, and the battle was for us. We, you and I, are God's gift to Jesus. If we hold onto our sins and refuse the forgiveness Jesus won for us, we are saying He died in vain; He shouldn't have bothered to die. Take the forgiveness Jesus died for you to have.

Tools for Battle-The Word is a Weapon

In Ephesians chapter 6 God says to put on the armor of God and take the sword of the Spirit which is the Word of God. The Word of God is powerful because it has the force of heaven behind it.

2 Corinthians 10: 3-5 *For though we live in the world, we do not wage war as the world does. The weapons we fight with are not the weapons of the world. On the contrary, they have divine power to demolish strongholds. We demolish arguments and every pretension that sets itself up against the knowledge of God, and we take captive every thought to make it obedient to Christ.*

The Word of God is sharper than any double-edged sword. So imagine what damage it is doing to the kingdom of darkness. No wonder the devil hates to hear it. Let's bother the devil today.

COMMAND those thoughts to leave in the name of Jesus.
 2 Corinthians 10:5 *We demolish arguments and every pretension that sets itself up against the knowledge of God, and we take captive every thought to make it obedient to Christ.*

Make your thoughts obey God. Just do it. Put your hands on your head and say "I COMMAND my thoughts into obedience." When you start obsessing or thinking that your husband is unfaithful or your children are going to get sick and die... put your hands on your head and command your mind. Say mind I command you to obey Jesus.

We Can Pray Scripture.

Much of Scripture is prayer. Did you know that we can use scripture and make it our own personal prayer? God's Word is true and perfect and a great way to pray. It shows God we believe in Him and His word and we believe His word is true and powerful. You can never pray wrong when you pray God's Word back to

Him. How can he refuse? When we pray God's Word, we know we are praying according to His will for us. Personalize the scripture by filling in your name or the name of the person you are praying for.

Psalm 91 is a great Scripture passage to pray. The whole Psalm is a prayer. I am including the first few verses and how to pray them below.

1 Whoever dwells in the shelter of the Most High will rest in the shadow of the Almighty.
- "Father I am yours and you are my shelter in the storm, I choose to rest in you."

2 I will say of the LORD, "He is my refuge and my fortress, my God, in whom I trust."
- "You Lord are my refuge, my fortress, nothing can hurt me. I trust you God."

3 Surely he will save you from the fowler's snare and from the deadly pestilence.
- "Surely You will save me from every trap the enemy sets for me, You will surely save me from sickness and disease and EVERY LITTLE THOUGHT that comes into my head. Thank you for keeping me from harm. I am not afraid of anything. Nothing can harm me because I am in your care."

Colossians 1:9-10 *We continually ask God to fill you with the knowledge of His will through all the wisdom and understanding that the Spirit gives... so that you may live a life worthy of the Lord and please him in every way: bearing fruit in every good work, growing in the knowledge of God,*

Pray this for a loved one.

- Prayer - God, I ask you to fill ___(fill in your daughter's name)___ with the knowledge of Your will. Give her wisdom and understanding so that _____ may live a life worthy of You Lord. I pray that _____ will please you in every way and that she will bear fruit as she works and grows in the knowledge of you, Lord.

All of Colossians is prayer. How serious are you? How much time to do you have? Make it your prayer and pray a couple verses a day.

Tools for Battle - Your Mouth is a Weapon

Speak to the Mountains/Strongholds

> **Mark 11:22-25** *"Have faith in God," Jesus answered. "Truly I tell you, if anyone says to this mountain, 'Go, throw yourself into the sea,' and does not doubt in their heart but believes that what they say will happen, it will be done for them. Therefore I tell you, whatever you ask for in prayer, believe that you have received it, and it will be yours. And when you stand praying, if you hold anything against anyone, forgive them, so that your Father in heaven may forgive you your sins."*

What mountain is in your way? What mountain is looming in your thought life, in your dreams? What mountain or mountains do you need to throw into the sea, never to be remembered or visited again? I don't mean the pretty, majestic mountains we all wished we lived next too. I mean those ugly, high, huge, overpowering, overcoming, overwhelming mountains or circumstances. They may be memories, disease, fear, worry, debt, finances, cancer, alcohol, addiction, anger, or unforgiveness. What mountain needs to be uprooted and thrown into the sea? Is it the memory of an event, a sin, depression, or marriage problems? What seems insurmountable or impossible? What is troubling you beyond your ability to conquer or overcome? Maybe your mountain is a bunch of things, and you can't quite name what is bothering you, you just feel oppressed. You feel dread, doom, as if something is looming over you.

A mountain is something we can't see over or around or get across to the other side. A mountain is something standing in your way to freedom and the good life Jesus promised. The mountain is always there. If it isn't in front of you, it is following behind you. You see it wherever you go; it's something you can't get away from. A mountain is a stronghold that needs to be demolished.

It's time to talk to our mountains. Jesus said "SAY to this

mountain." I once heard this, "We talk to God about how big our mountains are, but we should be talking to our mountains about how big our God is." So true. We talk to God and each other about how horrible our problems are when we should be talking to our problems about how great our God is! Let's refocus. Once we begin telling our problems what a great big God we have, our problems will seem small and manageable in comparison.

"Cancer, my God is greater, my God is stronger, my God is higher than you or anything you can throw at me, my God is healer, awesome in power and nothing is too difficult for Him."

Recite Psalm 18 to your problems then you will remember who is in control.

"The LORD is my rock, my fortress and my deliverer; my God is my rock, in whom I take refuge, my shield and the horn of my salvation, my stronghold. I called to the LORD, who is worthy of praise, and I have been saved from my enemies.

YOU CAN talk to your mountains. Jesus said so. Our words are powerful and can build up or destroy. No matter how big, how oppressive, how imposing, how ugly. You CAN talk and defeat that mountain of fear and move that mountain of insecurity. You may think you deserve that mountain of trouble, but it is time for it to go. You may have sinned and deserved the trouble you are going through, but you don't have to remain this way. Jesus came to take your sins and set you free from all it's consequences and guilt and shame.

Jesus said in **Mark 11:23** *"Have Faith in God." Jesus answered, "Truly I tell you, if anyone says to this mountain, 'Go, throw yourself into the sea,' and does not doubt in their heart but believes that what they say will happen, it will be done for them.*

Now let's practice. Tell it to throw itself into the sea.

"Insecurity go throw yourself into the sea"
"Fear go throw yourself into the sea"
"Depression go throw yourself into the sea"
"Sickness or disease go throw yourself into the sea"
"Resentment, bitterness, anxiety/worry, addictions,
     jealousy......go throw yourself into the sea!"

Now believe it!!! Jesus goes on to say *"Therefore I tell you, whatever you ask for in prayer, believe that you have received it, and it will be yours"* **Mark 11:24.**

Believe that God has heard your prayers. Believe that He is on your side, that He is fighting your battles for you. Believe that whatever you ask for in prayer you have received it. (see section on Faith)

Tools for Battle - Speak to Goliath

**Do You Have a Goliath That Needs to be Destroyed?
God doesn't play around with evil. He takes care of it.**

1 Samuel 17 is the story of David and Goliath. Goliath was the enemy, he and his army, the Philistines, were attacking the Israelites and the whole Israelite army was afraid of Goliath, and no one thought they could defeat him. Every day for 40 days the Philistines sent Goliath out to taunt the Israelites. He would shout at them and say "send someone to fight me. If I win you and your armies will serve us. If you win, we will be your servants."

All the Israelites were afraid of Goliath because they believed no one would be able to beat him. They had no confidence. When David showed up on the scene, he couldn't believe what he saw. He saw the whole Israelite army afraid of Goliath. He looked at them and how they reacted to Goliath. The Bible said, "they all fled from him (Goliath) in great fear." David, a youth, said "What? You are afraid of him, an uncircumcised man who defies the God of Israel?" David was like, "Really?Let me at him. I have taken care of the lion and the bear. God has protected me then, and he will protect me from this." David was amazed that the Israelite troops did not know who they were, who they belonged to, or where their protection came from. David was amazed that they did not recognize Goliath as an enemy of God.

Whoever comes against you, the King's child comes against the King himself.

David knew who His God was, he knew what His God was capable of, and he had no doubt that God would go before him. David knew that God would show up, he had no doubt. He was the only one who knew. No one else had faith that God was on their side. They doubted God would come through for them.

David knew just how big God was and just how small Goliath was. The Israelites saw Goliath as huge and themselves as small and insignificant against such an enemy. They saw the situation as impossible, but David had a different perspective, one that included GOD.

Do you know who you are? YOU are a child of the most high God. He is your father, and you are a coheir with Christ. You may not feel like it, but IT IS TRUE. You are a Christian. Being a Christian is not just a matter of getting something, or going somewhere, it's a matter of being someone. Someone special.

David's MOUNTAIN started talking to him. Goliath started talking to David. GOOD THING David didn't listen. David knew His God was bigger than his mountain.

> **1 Samuel 17:42** *He looked David over and saw that he was little more than a boy, glowing with health and handsome, and he despised him. 43 He said to David, "Am I a dog, that you come at me with sticks?" And the Philistine cursed David by his gods. 44 "Come here," he said, "and I'll give your flesh to the birds and the wild animals!"*

If you do not talk to Goliath or your mountains, they will talk to you. Your mountains will tell you lies all day and keep you up at night. Have you ever been up all night worrying? This is your mountain talking back to you. You have to be in charge and start speaking to your mountains and telling them where to go and who is in charge.

David didn't pay attention to Goliath. Instead, he answered him,

> *45 David said to the Philistine, "You come against me with sword and spear and javelin, but I come against you in the name of the LORD Almighty, the God of the armies of Israel, whom you have defied. 46 This day the LORD will*

> *deliver you into my hands, and I'll strike you down and cut off your head. This very day I will give the carcasses of the Philistine army to the birds and the wild animals, and the whole world will know that there is a God in Israel. 47 All those gathered here will know that it is not by sword or spear that the LORD saves; for the battle is the LORD's, and he will give all of you into our hands."*
>
> *48 As the Philistine moved closer to attack him, David ran quickly toward the battle line to meet him. 49 Reaching into his bag and taking out a stone, he slung it and struck the Philistine on the forehead. The stone sank into his forehead, and he fell facedown on the ground.*

So here is the word of God to use when you come up against your opponent, or your personal mountain, for example, depression. Let's say what David said.

> **I come against you** *depression* **in the name of the Lord almighty, In the name of Jesus whom you have defied. This day the Lord will deliver you** *depression* **into my hands and I will strike you down** *depression* **and cut off your head. This very day I will give the carcass of** *depression* **to the birds and the wild animals and the whole world will know that there is a God.**

REPEAT this with debt, sickness, whatever your stronghold is. **"I COME AGAINST YOU spirit of infirmity..."** If you still do not think you are allowed to speak and command, listen again to what Jesus says in **Luke 10:17-19** *"The seventy-two returned with joy and said, 'Lord, even the demons submit to us in your name.' He replied, 'I saw Satan fall like lightning from heaven. I have given you authority to trample on snakes and scorpions and to overcome all the power of the enemy; nothing will harm you.'"*

Every time the thoughts come we have an opportunity to speak to them. Our words are powerful; words can build up or destroy. We spend a lot of time saying, "I'm tired, I'm sick." We want people (especially our family members) to feel sorry for us; we say "I am going to die." We tell our friends how bad things are. We want them to know what we are going through; we want them to do something for us, to make it better, to save us. Why is it so easy to say "I am sick, or I am sick of this or that" instead of "I am so blessed" Let's spend some time saying the opposite. What do we have to lose?

Say, "I am well."

You may not feel well, but you are speaking faith in your God who heard your prayers. It's hard to break bad habits. We have made a habit of the way we talk. It takes practice. At first, it will sound weird saying the opposite of what you feel. But we are speaking forth truths based on God's Word, His promises to us, not on our feelings. The bible says to call forth those things that are not as though they are (Romans 4:17)! That is what we are doing. We are calling forth DECLARING what God says about us, what God's plan for us is, what God's will for us is, AS THOUGH IT was manifested right now. We are declaring our faith in God. We are declaring it to show Him we believe He is in control of the situation and fighting on our behalf.

Tools for Battle - Jesus is our Stronghold

Without Jesus, we are at the mercy of principalities, and spiritual forces of evil. With Jesus we are more than conquerors.

Our stronghold as Christians should be Jesus Christ. The word of God says "He is our stronghold." Our goal should be to make Jesus our stronghold. That must be the goal of every Christian; to be so wrapped up in Jesus and walking in the Holy Spirit that no weapon formed against us will prosper. We want to be immovable, unshakable, trustworthy, noble men and women of integrity; man and women of God. We invite you Holy Spirit. Only you can keep us in Christ. Help us to remain in Christ, Holy Spirit.

There may be an ongoing battle for us and for our minds, but with Jesus as our Lord, we win. Jesus is alive! Jesus is our Lord and Savior. Without Jesus as our Lord and Savior, we are at the mercy of principalities and spiritual forces of evil in the heavenly realms, yet we are more than conquerors with him. We can overcome anything. We are no longer trapped, no longer stuck and no longer enslaved, but free. Learn how and why do we need to make Jesus our Lord and Savior.

Personal Commitment
To Jesus as Lord and Savior

"Christianity did not begin with a theological formulation, a set of laws, or even a prayer form; it certainly did not begin with a document. It began with a person. Christianity is all about commitment to a person. The person of Jesus Christ. Jesus says, "Here I am, I stand at the door and knock if anyone hears my voice and opens the door, I will come in." This quote is from the Christ Renews His Parish (CRHP) Manual. The manual also says "The act of commitment is a prayer of self-offering which in simple terms expresses belief in Christ as Savior and Lord, acknowledges our sinfulness and need and clearly places our entire life in the hands of Jesus." It goes on to say "being a follower of Jesus is not a matter of birth, but of decision....The tradition of infant baptism claims the faith of the community for the infant, but expects each to choose Jesus for himself when he can do so."

You have to choose Jesus for yourself at some point.

My true conversion experience came when I was 28. At the time, I wanted to change the world; I thought I could make a difference in the world and be a champion for the poor. I expected so much more from my life than merely existing and accumulating wealth and I was filled with guilt and shame. I thought I should be in the peace corp or on the mission field instead of making money and spending it on myself. I was racked with guilt. One night God met me and spoke to me. I knew it was God. He said, "Come to me first and then you will have the power."

He said, "Come to me first and then you will have the power."

It was as if all of a sudden the lights went on. Those amazing words from God opened my eyes to His awesome greatness and love for me for the first time. I had grown up Catholic, went to Catholic schools and received all the sacraments with knowledge and enthusiasm and genuinely loved God. But that day I surrendered my life to him. All my life I was trying to do good and earn his love but all he wanted was me. The reality of that is still being revealed to me to this day. He wanted ME, and he wanted me just the way I was. He didn't expect me to come to Him all clean and pretty. He wanted me just the way I was full of sins and all. He was willing to invest in me because I am worth it. I matter to Him. He will take a lifetime to clean me up and mold me into His image.

That night He stood at the door of my heart and knocked, and I opened it. He made it so clear to me as if He was saying, "your itty bitty way or MINE." I realized in that instant that I was trying to accomplish on my own, was possible only with Him. What a partnership He was offering me. That night the God of the universe, the omnipotent all powerful God was standing at the door of my heart waiting for my response (little ole' me). God considered me worthy of His time and attention. My response was a resounding YES. That night I was forever changed because I made a commitment to Him.

Jesus is here right now and is calling you. You are not reading this by accident. Jesus is saying, *"Here I am, I stand at the door and knock. If anyone hears my voice and opens the door I will come in."* **(Rev. 3:20)**

We can make a commitment to our church, to our community, to the poor and even to those in prison but it will not gain us anything in the sight of God without a personal commitment to Jesus Christ, His Son, our Lord, and Savior.

So what does it mean to accept Jesus as Lord and Savior? First, what does it mean to make Jesus Lord?

Jesus As Lord

God made Jesus Lord of heaven and earth because Jesus lowered himself to accept death, death on a cross, and therefore, God exalted him as Lord. The Bible says that *at the name of Jesus every knee shall bow and every tongue proclaim Jesus Christ is Lord* **(From Philippians 2:8-10).** It will happen one day. One day everyone will bow, better now than later when it's too late.

When we commit to Jesus as Lord, we surrender our right to do things our way. He becomes Lord; He is in control. His way for our way. What an exchange. The perfect for the imperfect. We are billions of beings walking around on earth in charge of our own lives thinking we know what is best for us. The problem is, everybody has a different idea and formula for life. God is saying to each of us on earth, "Here I am, ask me, I know." God is perfect, and His will for our lives is perfect. What do we get in return? Everything! All God's promises are ours. Jesus said in **Matthew 6:33** *"Seek first the Kingdom of heaven and His righteousness and all these things will be added to you as well."* Everything you need and desire God will provide for you.

With Jesus as Lord, all things are ours. We have peace, joy, and freedom. The Bible says that whoever the Son sets free, is free indeed. We are free from depression, oppression, from the power and enslavement of addictions, free from the past, free from generational sin. If your past haunts you, you have the opportunity in Christ to begin again. No matter how old you are, no matter how long you have done things your way, you have the opportunity to begin again. The Holy Spirit gives you the power to do it. The Holy Spirit gives you the power to commit your life to Jesus. The Holy Spirit gives us the power to live for Him also. He doesn't leave us on our own.

Often we hear," I came home to the church," or "I finally came back to the church or found church for the first time." But salvation is found in Jesus Christ not in a church building and not in a denomination, but in the person of Jesus Christ. We worship Jesus, not a church. When we come to Jesus as our Lord, our whole life will be turned around, true healing, forgiveness, freedom and life is ours. Jesus says,*"I came that they may have life and have it abundantly."***(John 10:10)** He wasn't lying. His way leads us to the good life. It is ours, and He is not keeping it from us but offering it to us here on earth. We can trust Him as Lord because He is faithful and true, perfect and trustworthy.

Jesus said **(John 15:5)** *"Apart from me you can do nothing."* The bible also says in **Galatians 2:21** *If righteousness* *could be gained through the law than Christ died for nothing.* If we can be made right with God by obeying all the commandments, then Christ died for nothing. Which brings me to the reason we need Jesus as our Savior.

Jesus As Savior

We want to be righteous, we want to be made right with God, but we can't do it on our own. That is why we need a savior, and that is why God sent His son. God knew we needed a Savior. When we accept Jesus as Savior, we accept that what He did on the cross was for us personally. We believe that our sins are on Him. You have an opportunity to make a radical decision for Christ that will forever change your life. For some of us that may have already happened. God made a covenant with us and signed it with the blood of Jesus. *"This cup is the new covenant in my blood which is poured out for you"* **Luke 22:20**. Jesus gave it all for us, and now He stands at the door and knocks.

Tools for Battle - Praise is a Weapon

***2 Chronicles 20:22** "As they began to sing and praise, the LORD set ambushes against the men of Ammon and Moab and Mount Seir who were invading Judah, and they were defeated."*

In 2 Chronicles, King Jehoshaphat fought the armies coming against him with praise and worship. Joshua conquered Jericho with a shout. Joshua and his armies walked around the city praising God, and with one shout the walls around the city fell. God is trying to tell us something. God wages war differently. Let's learn to praise God. In Psalms, the Lord commands us to praise Him because our praise has the power to defeat the enemy.

See **Psalm 66:1-4** and **Psalm 145:1-4**

What does it mean to PRAISE GOD? The dictionary defines praise as "to commend (*Tell others about God, who He is or what He has done for you*), to applaud, to express approval of, or admiration of, to extol in words or song, to magnify, to glorify, to exalt."

I don't think THERE IS anything more pleasing to GOD than to hear HIS PEOPLE SINGING PRAISE TO HIM, especially as one body. God loves to hear you sing to him. God loves to hear us praise him. Do you want to make God happy? Start praising him. Do you want to see the atmosphere around you change, start praising God? If you don't know how to or what to say start with the Psalms listed below or the Praise Statements or Litany of Praise in the pages to follow.

When we praise God, we are telling him we understand who he is and what he has done for us. Our praise shows God our devotion, love and trust in His power and goodness and His desire to save, protect and take care of us. We show Him we believe and accept his LORDSHIP!!! It's huge. When we praise God for who He is and for what He has done, we prove to God we know what He has done and who He is. When I think of what Jesus did for me, I can't help but praise His holy name.

Psalm 95:1-3
Come, let us sing for joy to the LORD; let us shout aloud to the Rock of our salvation. Let us come before him with thanksgiving and extol him with music and song. For the LORD is the great God, the great King above all gods.

Psalm 150: 1-6
Hallelujah!
Praise God in his holy sanctuary; give praise in the mighty dome of heaven. Give praise for his mighty deeds, praise him for his great majesty. Give praise with blasts upon the horn, praise him with harp and lyre. Give praise with tambourines and dance, praise him with strings and pipes. Give praise with crashing cymbals, praise him with sounding cymbals. Let everything that has breath give praise to the LORD! Hallelujah!

Praise is being preoccupied with GOD; with who He is and what He has done. **Praise is** raising much ado about God.
Praise is giving God the GLORY.

P R A I S E

P	Physical, clapping, raising hands, someone should recognize or notice that you are praising God
R	Raising hands as a gesture
A	Any time, anywhere, always
I	Intentional
S	Song
E	Expressed

Psalm 66:8 says to let His praises be heard. Praise is not "praise" until it is vocalized. You can't praise your husband or your children by thinking it. They just won't get the benefit until you actually say it. For some reason, it is easier to criticize than to applaud or express admiration and approval. Praising God does

not come naturally to us, but complaining does. We have to work at praise; it takes practice commitment and discipline.

I love Pam Criss's teaching on Praise, this is an excerpt..

WHY PRAISE GOD - Pam Criss

So the question is why do we give God the Glory? We do it because God instructs us to as we've just heard in scripture, because that is why God created us and also, very simply, because HE deserves it. The great thing about giving God the Glory and Praise is it takes our eyes off of ourselves and onto Him, the place where our gaze should always be. When we look up, we magnify God, the creator of heaven and earth, our Lord and King.

I'm sure we've all personally experienced or know someone who has experienced significant pain and suffering. People who don't know the Lord often tailspin when faced with a crisis. Those who have their trust in the Lord persevere. Regardless of the circumstances, they are safe in God's arms, with the faith and knowledge that God is God and knows more than we do. Your life will be in proper order and perspective when you put God first; everything will just fall into place and be aligned correctly. People who put God in the backseat and only call on Him in time of crisis truly have it all backward.

Famous author and once atheist, C.S. Lewis, said "Aim at heaven and you'll get earth thrown in. Aim at earth, and you'll get neither." So then the question becomes HOW do we give God the glory He deserves? Truthfully I don't think we ever can, but I believe we should die trying.

We need to give Him thanks for all our blessings; give Him the glory for love and creation and for all that is good.

Philippians 4:8 *"Finally, brothers, whatever is true, whatever is honorable, whatever is just, whatever is pure, whatever is lovely, whatever is gracious, if there is any excellence and if there is anything worthy of praise, think about these things."*

In **John 10:10** Jesus says *"A thief comes only to steal and slaughter and destroy; I come so that they might have life and have it more abundantly."*

God doesn't want us to live our lives sad or depressed or sick or with an addiction. He wants us to live abundantly in Him.

When we have our eyes on God it suddenly doesn't make our situation seem so significant or overwhelming. When we praise God with our voice, our mind will follow. It's hard to stay down when you are singing about how great your God is. Try it. Try repeating the following words of praise and see.

"God, you are all powerful, ever-living and ever loving. You are God of all gods and Lord of all Lords. You are the everlasting God, the maker of heaven and earth. Nothing is too difficult for you."

When you begin to tell God how big and powerful and great He is, all of sudden your problems seem small in comparison. When you praise God, your focus is diverted from you and your problems to God and his ability to answer. God says in ***Psalm 29:1 and 2 "Give to the Lord, you heavenly beings, give to the Lord glory and might; Give to the Lord the glory due God's name. Bow down before the Lord's holy splendor."***

Webster defines GLORY as very great praise, honor or distinction bestowed by common consent. Also, adoring praise or worshipful thanksgiving. Another way to define GLORY is to give credit where credit is due.

A worldly example that I think we can all relate to is if someone makes a game winning shot at a basketball game, that person often gets the glory for winning the game. And how easy that is for us, to give a basketball player GLORY?

Giving God the due Glory or praise He deserves should come naturally to us, but it often goes against what we learn in this world, which is too-often self-centered and material. I believe the key to giving God glory, or giving God praise is we have to ASK God for what we want and need so that He has the opportunity to answer us and then we can give Him the glory and praise He deserves.

In the Bible it tells us over and over and over again to ASK. Bring your concerns and burdens to God. ASK and let God take it from there. Yet for some reason when we are faced with a trial, a sick child, a boss who is impossible to work with or a failing marriage we try to go it alone. We may talk to our family and friends, read the latest books, or go for counseling, but If we don't take it to God, we don't give God the

opportunity to answer our prayers.
We do not have, because we do not ask! That's right; we have not because we ask not!

I did a quick Google search on where in the Bible it says for us to ASK. The result was three pages long, but I wanted to share with you a few of my favorite scripture verses where it says to ASK.

Luke 11:9 and 10 *And I tell you, ask and you will receive; seek and you will find; knock and the door will be opened to you. For every one who asks, receives; and the one who seeks, finds; and to the one who knocks, the door will be opened.*

1 Kings 3:5 *In Gibeon the Lord appeared to Solomon in a dream at night. God said, Ask something of me and I will give to you.*

Matthew 21:22 *Whatever you ask for in prayer with faith, you will receive.*

John 14:13-14 *And whatever you ask in my name, I will do it, so that theFather may be glorified in the son. If you ask anything of me in my name, I will do it.*

John 15:7 *If you remain in me and my words remain in you, ask for whatever you want and it will be done for you.*

James 4:2b *You do not possess because you do not ask.*

John 16:23 and 24 *On that day you will not question me about anything. Amen, amen I say to you, whatever you ask the Father in my name He will give you. Until now you have not asked anything in my name; ask and you will receive, so that your joy may be complete.*

James 1:5 and 6 *But if any of you lacks wisdom, he should ASK God who gives to all generously and ungrudgingly, and he will be given it. But he should ask in faith, not doubting, for the one who doubts is like a wave of the sea that is driven and tossed about by the wind.*

We don't like asking. We think for some reason we are bothering God. Why is asking so important? When we ask for something from God, and He gives it to us, or He does it, we can tell everyone all about it. Then God gets all the glory.

Pam Criss

Praise as a Sacrifice

Psalm 50:14 *Offer praise as your sacrifice to God; fulfill your vows to the Most High.* **Psalm 50:23** - *Those who offer praise as a sacrifice honor me.*

Sacrifice means giving something you treasure or prize for the sake of a higher calling. Sacrifice is something we do for the Lord. We do it just because He is Lord. Sacrifice is something we offer up. My mother used to tell us all the time "offer it up," referring to something we had to do that we didn't really want to do. When you offer something up for the sake of another, you do it whether you feel like it or not.

When we bring a sacrifice of praise to our Lord Jesus (in the form of song or dance or clapping or telling someone about him) we are telling Him that He is worth our praise and worship, whether we feel like it or not. How much more do you think He appreciates us and our efforts when we do it even when we don't want to or when we don't feel like it. God notices when we praise even though we might look foolish, or our voices are pitiful and off key.

Hebrews 13:15 *Through Jesus, therefore, let us continually offer to God a sacrifice of praise—the fruit of lips that openly profess his name.*

This is what we do when we sing praises. In the Old Testament, the Hebrews offered sacrifices of bulls, goats, calves, grain, and the first fruits of the harvest. They offered their best. The unblemished lambs. The Lord tells us to praise him with song and with music over and over in the Bible. Let's do it and let's give Him our best. He is worth our time, our effort, and our attention.

Praise Statements / Scriptures

SAY THESE OUT LOUD as a way to express your praise to God You may respond ***"Praise you Jesus"*** or ***"Thank you Lord"***.

You are the everlasting God, the creator of all things. The creator of the universe.

You are our hope, we trust You in everything and always.

You never let us down, we can count on you.
You never fail us. You are our Father who loves us.

We depend on you Lord Jesus because you are dependable. You are faithful and true to your Word.

Our future is in your hands, you promise us a future full of hope. You promise that your children will not have to beg for bread so we trust you for our daily bread, both now and forever. We will not fear.

You are the ever-loving and ever-living God.

You never give up on us, you never grow tired or weary.

You are our provider, you supply all our needs.

You are the King of Kings, and Lord of all Lords. The Great I am.

You are all powerful, nothing is too difficult for you.
With you ALL THINGS are possible.

Everything is possible for Him who believes.

We are more than conquerors through You Lord Jesus.

You are our ever-present help in time of need.

Lord You are compassionate and gracious, slow to anger, abounding in love.

You will never leave us nor forsake us.

You LORD take delight in us;
You crown the humble with victory.

You are our defender. Our Strong Tower, our mighty fortress. No weapon formed against us can stand.

If God is for us who can be against us.

You redeem our life from the pit and crown me with love and compassion.

You satisfy my desires with good things so that my youth is renewed like the eagle'.

You move mountains for us, Lord,
You move heaven and earth for us, your children.

You do not treat us as our sins deserve or repay us according to our iniquities. For as high as the heavens are above the earth, so great is Your love for us who fear You; as far as the east is from the west, You have removed our transgressions from us.

We are your children, heirs in your kingdom.

You are our great warrior. We never fight our battles alone. You are our armor, our shield, our great protection.

You are the author of life, in You we live, move and have our being.

You are the Alpha and the Omega, the first and the last. The beginning and the end.

You preserve our lives and keep our feet from slipping. You guard us and watch over us. You command your angels to protect us.

Truly my soul finds rest in God; my salvation comes from Him. Truly He is my rock and my salvation; He is my fortress, I will never be shaken.

Lord you are the Balm of Gilead. Our healer.

We can do all things through You Lord Jesus. You are our strength, and our champion.

You are the way to the Father, we come boldly to the throne of grace because You bore our sins.

You bore our sins and carried our diseases. By Your stripes we are healed.

We are free from sin because of the price You paid.

I am forgiven, Jesus did not die in vain. We walk in confidence and victory because You took our shame and the penalty due us.

You are the Font of all holiness. You are the living water.

Rivers of living water flow out of me because the Holy Spirit lives in me.

The same Spirit that raised Jesus from the dead lives in me.

Jesus came to destroy the works of the devil. He is our deliverer. He delivers us from every evil.

He is the vine, we are the branches, without Him we can do nothing.

Jesus, You are the Bread of Life, my sustenance.

You are my safety, my refuge, my God in whom I trust. He delivers me from all my fears and saves me from all my troubles.

Though the earth be shaken and the mountains quake, though the waters rage and foam and the mountains fall, I do not fear. The Lord of Hosts is with me.

Praise be to God, who has not rejected my prayer or withheld His love from me.

Lord I trust you completely because you are trustworthy. You are my Lord, my God and my King.

LITANY OF PRAISE

Praise You, Jesus, You are my life, my love.
Praise You, Jesus, You are the name above all names.
Praise You, Jesus, You are Emmanuel, God with us.
Praise You, Jesus, You are the King of Kings.
Praise You, Jesus, You are the King of creation.
Praise You, Jesus, You are King of the universe.
Praise You, Jesus, You are the Lord of lords.
Praise You, Jesus, You are the Almighty.
Praise You, Jesus, You are the Christ. Christ the King.
Praise You, Jesus, You are the Lamb of God.
Praise You, Jesus, You are Lion of Judah.
Praise You, Jesus, You are the Bright Morning Star.
Praise You, Jesus, You are our Champion and shield.
Praise You, Jesus, You are our Strength and our Song.
Praise You, Jesus, You are the way of our life.
Praise You, Jesus, You are the only truth.
Praise You, Jesus, You are the real life.
Praise You, Jesus, You are the Wonderful Counselor.
Praise You, Jesus, You are the Prince of Peace.
Praise You, Jesus, You are the Light of the World.
Praise You, Jesus, You are the Living Word.
Praise You, Jesus, You are the Redeemer.
Praise You, Jesus, You are the Anointed One.
Praise You, Jesus, You are the Holy one of Israel.
Praise You, Jesus, You are the Good Sheperd.
Praise You, Jesus, You are the Sheepgate.
Praise You, Jesus, You are the Lord of hosts.
Praise You, Jesus, You are the Rock of all ages.
Praise You, Jesus, You are my hiding place.
Praise You, Jesus, You are the Savior of the world.
Praise You, Jesus, You are the strong tower.
Praise You, Jesus, You are the Mountain Refuge.
Praise You, Jesus, You are the Bread of Life.
Praise You, Jesus, You are the Font of all holiness.

Praise You, Jesus, You are the Living Water.
Praise You, Jesus, You are the True Vine.
Praise You, Jesus, You are my Spouse. my Maker.
Praise You, Jesus, You are our Fortress.
Praise You, Jesus, You are the Deliverer.
Praise You, Jesus, You are our Victory.
Praise You, Jesus, You are our Salvation.
Praise You, Jesus, You are our Righteousness.
Praise You, Jesus, You are our Wisdom.
Praise You, Jesus, You are our Sanctification.
Praise You, Jesus, You are our Justification.
Praise You, Jesus, You are the Door.
Praise You, Jesus, You are the great I AM.
Praise You, Jesus, You are the great High Priest.
Praise You, Jesus, You are the Cornerstone.
Praise You, Jesus, You are the Sure Foundation.
Praise You, Jesus, You are our Joy. Our Portion and Cup.
Praise You, Jesus, You are my Healing and Wholeness.
Praise You, Jesus, You are our Covenant.
Praise You, Jesus, You are the Promise of the Father.
Praise You, Jesus, You are the Everlasting One.
Praise You, Jesus, You are the Most High God.
Praise You, Jesus, You are the Lamb that was slain.
Praise You, Jesus, You are the Just Judge.
Praise You, Jesus, You are the Balm of Gilead.
Praise You, Jesus, You are the Mighty Warrior.
Praise You, Jesus, You are my Defense.
Praise You, Jesus, You are the Bridegroom.
Praise You, Jesus, You are my Patience.
Praise You, Jesus, You are the Solid Reality
Praise You, Jesus, You are my Provider.
Praise You, Jesus, You are the Resurrection and the Life.
Praise You, Jesus, You are the Alpha and the Omega.
Praise You, Jesus, You are the Beginning and the End.
Praise You, Jesus, You are all that I need, and all that I want.
Praise You, Jesus, You are worthy of all praise.   Amen

Healing

Isaiah 53:5 *But he was pierced for our transgressions, he was crushed for our iniquities; the punishment that brought us peace was on him, and by his wounds we are healed.*

Matthew 8: 16-17 *When evening came, many who were demon-possessed were brought to him, and he drove out the spirits with a word and healed all the sick. This was to fulfill what was spoken through the prophet Isaiah: "He took up our infirmities and bore our diseases."*

I believe that Jesus heals today just like yesterday. Jesus hasn't changed. He is still alive and sitting at the right hand of God forever interceding on our behalf. As a matter of fact, Jesus never said no to anyone. Everyone was healed who asked Him or came to Him for healing. God wants to heal you. I can tell that till I am blue in the face, but it takes you getting into the word of God with the help of the Holy Spirit to see this for yourself. Faith is believing God wants to heal you.

I used to have this plaque in my home above the door that read "Faith is not believing God can, but that God will." Anyone can believe God can. It doesn't require faith to believe God can; even the devil believes that. Faith is required to believe he will. HE WILL! HE wants to heal you more than you want to be healed. Yes!

This next excerpt on healing from my friend Pam Criss, she writes....

> I say, ask God for everything—to take your headache away, for a good parking spot, to help your child ace the TAKS test, the raise you've been waiting for, etc. etc. etc. And be very specific in your prayer request so that you will truly KNOW that it's GOD who is answering. For example, don't just pray for

marriages in general. Pray for your marriage and any marriage you know of that needs prayer, but specifically name them and their needs.

Years ago I heard a CEO comment on what surprised her most about her job. She said it was when she gave her employees their reviews she would ask them what they wanted for a raise and 9/10 times they would ask for less than she was willing to give them! Wow, if they had only known. So in life, I say, pray and ask big. Think about it…when we find out someone is sick what do we typically pray for? So often we pray for the person to have the strength to endure the illness, for patience, for their family.

We don't ask for healing—we don't go for the miracle! The general thinking is if the person is sick then God's will must be for the person to be ill and we certainly don't want to go against God's will. But just as Scripture says, we are called to ASK. To the person who says "what if it's not God's will to heal the person?" I say, "what if it is? What if God is just waiting for someone to ask Him?" God is a gentleman. So when people ask me to pray for them, and they are sick, I always ask for complete healing. If it's a situation that the doctor's say the person can't be healed, I think, OK it's going to be easier for God to get the glory on this one when the person is healed. There was a lady in my Bible study group whose son's eardrum shattered and the doctor said he'll never hear out of that ear again. But we didn't stop praying for him after that diagnosis. And you know what, his hearing has slightly started to return, praise be to God, and we are continuing to pray for complete restoration of that ear!

My Bible lists Jesus' miracles in chronological order—of the 35 miracles, 27 were regarding HEALING. When Jesus was here on Earth people constantly came to Him for healing and He never once turned anyone away. Think about that—He healed everyone who asked. And I believe He will do the same for us today. In Pope Benedict XVI new book <u>Jesus of Nazareth</u> he

> says of Jesus "He does not come bearing the sword of the revolutionary. He comes with the gift of healing."Healing our bodies, souls, spirits, our marriages, families, friendships, neighbors, countries and yes our world.
> **Pam Criss**

May I reiterate what Pam said about general prayers. Steer away from general prayers; the HOLY SPIRIT will help you. They lack faith and therefore are generally ineffective. Be specific, go for it. It is hard, but be daring. It is much easier to ask for strength or for healing or for help. It is much harder to ask for something specific (especially out loud). We worry and think, what if it doesn't happen. We are afraid of failure or making God look bad. Let God worry about God.

Most of the time we don't ask for specific things because we lack faith. "God may not want that for me" or "God has better things to do than to worry about my daughter's acne or my headache." I remember a man named John who came by one evening during Bible study needing prayer and I offered to pray with him. He said, "I was just diagnosed with stage 4 cancer." I got help from my friends, and we all held hands and began to pray. All of a sudden I felt the Holy Spirit urging me and I said "John did you know that in all the gospel, throughout the gospels, no one ever asked Jesus to give them strength. NEVER! They always asked for the healing." Jesus would say "what do you want?" and their responses would vary, "Lord heal my daughter," "I want to see," "I want to walk."

No one ever said to Jesus leave me the way I am, just give me the strength to get through it. But that is how we pray. We are so afraid God won't do it that we don't even want to ask. He said to me "Yes, Yes, that is all I want. I just want the strength to get through this." I realized that He did not hear what I was saying. Before I could think, before I could evaluate the words coming into my head I blurted out. "Well, I say stage 4 to stage zero in the Name of Jesus." I didn't hear from him until someone from church came to me and asked me if I had heard about John. He received good news from the Doctor, and he believes it was because God heard our prayer. When I ran into John on Easter Sunday, we praised God together.

God doesn't have any favorites!
Jesus came bearing gifts of healing and deliverance, and He gave them away freely and generously. He gave then, and He is still giving now. He does not have favorites. He does not love the leper in Matthew chapter 8 more than you. He doesn't love the blind man, the lame, the beggar, the paralytic, the demoniac, the Centurion's servant, the daughter of the Canaanite woman, the woman with the issue of blood or the countless others in the gospels more than you. The Bible says that our God is the the God that heals. Healing is a gift that needs to be received, opened and administered. Jesus said, you will recognize a believer when they lay hands on the sick, and the sick are healed.

Mark 9:23 says EVERYTHING IS possible for him who believes.

Mark 10:27 says that ALL THINGS are possible for God

Romans 10:17 Thus faith comes from what is heard, and what is heard comes through the word of Christ.

I find after just a few minutes of reading God's word I am filled with faith. Try it. Don't give up too quickly.
Call on the Holy Spirit to open the word for you.
Get ready to go places in the Spirit you have never been before and to keep on going. Make this your daily manna.

2 Corinthians 5:7 says "For we live by faith, not by sight. "
Remember let's not trust in our feelings or what it looks like.
We trust not in what we see but we are believers and we walk by faith.

Are you ready to go into the world filled with faith in God and making a difference in someone else's life.

Mark 16:18 "they will pick up snakes with their hands; and when they drink deadly poison, it will not hurt them at all; they will place their hands on sick people, and they will get well."

Daily Proclamations

Say any or all of these daily. These are declarations of faith. We are declaring what is not, as though it is. We do this because we have faith in the one we are counting on with our prayers. We have faith that God is hearing and answering our prayers. This is an excerpt from Kate Johnston on declaring in faith.

> "Declaring what is not, as though it is, by faith"
> This is a huge statement. When I first read it, I didn't understand what it meant. But when I broke it down, I could see what an important statement this really is. HOW can you tell your husband, "you're the best, or I love you totally till the day I die, or I couldn't have chosen a better husband or father than you"...how can you say this, when you don't FEEL that way at that time. And that's the point, we do not have to FEEL, but just BELIEVE with eyes of faith. We can declare what is not, because we're standing on His promise. We're standing on His word believing that He is fighting for us, He is doing a work in our husbands that we don't see. He is fighting our battles. We are BELIEVING in that promise.
>
> BELIEVE when you don't see...   that's FAITH
> (Kate Johnston Husband Challenge, 2010)

I command my thoughts into obedience. I put my mind on God. My mind is my property and mine to direct. I command every thought into obedience. Jesus, you are Lord of my mind, my thoughts and my emotions. I give my mind to you. I trust you. I choose to think on your thoughts. I come against any thought that is not of you. I reject evil thoughts and imaginations in the name of Jesus...

Phil 4:8 *Finally, brothers, whatever is true, whatever is honorable, whatever is just, whatever is pure, whatever is lovely, whatever is gracious, if there is any excellence and if there is anything worthy of praise, think about these things."*

I am valuable, and I am special to God. I have great worth, and my worth is not based on what others think of me nor does it depend on what I accomplish or how I perform. Jesus Christ himself gave His life for me and placed great value on me. I am deeply loved, pleasing, totally accepted and forgiven and free, brand new, complete and whole in Christ.

Jesus, I trust You, You care for me, You care about me. You are for me and not against me. You know me, my every thought and my motives and still, you love me with a love that will never change. I am yours, and I am safe. Nothing can hurt me. You are my ever present help in time of need. You are my father, and I run to you.

I will run and not grow weary; I will walk and not be faint. My future is secure. You have a plan in mind for me and a future full of hope. I will not fear or worry, but I choose to trust you with my life and my future. I am strong in the Lord and in His mighty Power. I can do all things through Christ who strengthens me. I am more than a conqueror through Him who loves me. I can overcome anything because Jesus will never leave me. He loves me just the way I am.

Jesus I am well, Your word says "By Your wounds, I am healed." I receive your love and healing and thank you for doing it for me. Sickness and disease, my God, is greater, my God is stronger, my God is higher than you or anything you can throw at me. My God is my healer, awesome in power and nothing is too difficult for Him. You took my sins, sickness, and disease to the cross. I accept this gift and believe it is mine. I choose to walk by faith and not by sight. I choose to believe you are healing me. Your word says that You took our infirmities with you to the cross and it says that You bore our diseases also on that same cross. I know you did that for me. Faith is not believing God can, but that God will. I believe Lord help me with my unbelief.

The following may take more faith than you have right now. Say it anyway. Watch your faith grow, and your husband become the man God created him to be.
SAY OUT LOUD....
My husband is a man after God's own heart.
My husband loves me; he is selfless, content, generous, loving and kind. My husband puts his wife and children first. My husband is God's problem, not mine. My husband is faithful and true. He is trustworthy. He is a good husband, and we are one in mind, body, and spirit. I love him and choose him.

My wife is beautiful and loving and a good mother. I love her and will cherish her all the days of my life. She is mine forever. She is a gift and loves me and wants only the best for me. She is hard working and trustworthy, patient and kind. I choose her.

I come against you, depression, in the name of the Lord Almighty, In the name of Jesus whom you have defied. This day the Lord will deliver you depression into my hands, and I will strike you down and cut off your head. This very day I will give the carcass of depression to the birds, and the wild animals and the whole world will know that there is a God.

Psalm 18 *The LORD is my rock, my fortress and my deliverer; my God is my rock, in whom I take refuge, my shield and the horn of my salvation, my stronghold. I called to the LORD, who is worthy of praise, and I have been saved from my enemies.*

Psalm 91

Whoever dwells in the shelter of the Most High
will rest in the shadow of the Almighty. I will say of the LORD,
"He is my refuge and my fortress, my God, in whom I trust."
Surely he will save you from the fowler's snare and from the
deadly pestilence. He will cover you with his feathers, and under
his wings you will find refuge; his faithfulness will be your shield
and rampart.

 You will not fear the terror of night, nor the arrow that flies by
day, nor the pestilence that stalks in the darkness, nor the plague
that destroys at midday. A thousand may fall at your side, ten
thousand at your right hand, but it will not come near you. You
will only observe with your eyes and see the punishment of the
wicked. If you say, "The LORD is my refuge," and you make the
Most High your dwelling, no harm will overtake you, no disaster
will come near your tent. For he will command his angels
concerning you to guard you in all your ways; they will lift you up
in their hands, so that you will not strike your foot against a stone.
You will tread on the lion and the cobra; you will trample the great
lion and the serpent. "Because he loves me," says the LORD, "I
will rescue him; I will protect him, for he acknowledges my name.
He will call on me, and I will answer him; I will be with him in
trouble, I will deliver him and honor him. With long life I will
satisfy him and show him my salvation."

God made a covenant with us and signed it
with the blood of Jesus.
"This cup is the new covenant in my blood which is poured out
for you." Jesus gave it all for us and
He stands at the door and knocks.

Prayer of Commitment

Jesus, I believe in You,
I believe you are the Son of God, and I believe You
died to free me from my sins. I believe You rose from
the dead to bring ME new life. Here I am Lord. Thank
you for taking me just the way I am. Thank you for
loving me just as I am. Lord Jesus, I want to belong to
You from now on. Take possession of me, forgive me,
free me from all darkness and evil. I trust You to heal
me and transform me into your disciple.

Prayer of Surrender

Today I surrender to You Lord Jesus. I surrender to
You because I trust You. I surrender all to You, my
health, my family, my finances, my work, my
relationships, my successes, and failures. I release it all
to You.
I surrender to You Lord, my fears, my insecurities, the
past, the present, and the future. I belong to You

To order more books go to
www.where2ormoregather.com/booksbible-studies/
or email mbwuenschel@gmail.com

Made in the USA
San Bernardino, CA
08 March 2017